I. The Problem in a Nutshell

Something that can't go on forever, won't.
Economist Herbert Stein

THE BUYERS think what they're buying will appreciate in value, making them rich in the future. The product grows more and more elaborate – and more and more expensive – but the expense is offset by cheap credit provided by sellers who are eager to encourage buyers to buy.

Buyers see that everyone else is taking on mounds of debt, and they are more comfortable when they do so themselves. Besides, for a generation, the value of what they buy has gone up steadily. What could go wrong? Everything continues smoothly until, at some point, it doesn't anymore.

Yes, this sounds like the housing bubble, but I'm afraid it's also sounding a lot like a still-inflating higher education bubble. And despite (or because of) the fact that my day job involves higher education, I think it's better for us to face up to what's going on *before* the bubble bursts messily. Because that's what's likely to happen.

No one disputes that college has gotten a lot more expensive. A recent *Money* magazine report notes, "After adjusting for financial aid, the amount families pay for college has skyrocketed 439 percent since 1982.... Normal supply and demand can't begin to explain cost increases of this magnitude." Consumers would balk, except for two things.

First – as with the housing bubble – cheap and readily available credit has let people borrow to finance education. They're willing to do so because of (1) consumer ignorance, as students – and, often, their parents – don't fully grasp just how harsh the impact of student-loan payments will be after graduation; and (2) a belief that whatever the cost, a college education is a necessary ticket to future prosperity.

Bubbles form when too many people expect values to go up forever. Bubbles burst when there are no longer enough excessively optimistic and ignorant folks to fuel them. And there are signs that this is beginning to happen already where education is concerned.

A recent *New York Times* profile featured Courtney Munna, a 26-year-old graduate of New York University with nearly $100,000

Bubbles form when too many people expect values to go up forever. Bubbles burst when there are no longer enough excessively optimistic and ignorant folks to fuel them.

---

in student-loan debt – debt that her degree in religious and women's studies did not equip her to repay. Payments on the debt are about $700 per month, equivalent to a respectable house payment and a major bite on her monthly income of $2,300 as a photographer's assistant earning an hourly wage. And, unlike a bad mortgage on an underwater house, Munna can't simply walk away from her student loans, which cannot be expunged in bankruptcy. She's stuck in a financial trap.

Some might say that she deserves it: Who borrows $100,000 to finance a degree in women's and religious studies that won't make you any money? She should have wised up, and others should learn from her mistake instead of learning too late, as she did: "I don't want to spend the rest of my life slaving away to pay for an education I got for four years and would happily give back."

But bubbles burst when people catch on, and there's some evidence that people are beginning to catch on. Student-loan demand, according to a recent report in *The Washington Post*, is going soft, and students are expressing a willingness to go to a cheaper school rather than run up debt. Things haven't collapsed yet, but they're looking shakier – kind of like the housing market looked in 2007.

So what happens if the bubble collapses? Will it be a tragedy, with millions of Americans losing their path to higher-paying jobs?

Maybe not. College is often described as a path to prosperity, but is it? A college education can help people make more money in three ways.

First, it may actually make them more economically productive by teaching them skills valued in the workplace: computer programming, nursing, or engineering, say. (Religious and women's studies, not so much.)

Second, it may provide a credential that employers want, not because it represents actual skills but because it's a weeding tool that doesn't produce civil-rights suits as, say, IQ tests might. A four-year college degree, even if its holder acquired no actual skills, at least indicates some ability to show up on time and perform as instructed.

And third, a college degree – at least an elite one – may hook its holder up with a useful social network that can provide jobs and opportunities in the future. (This is truer if it's a degree from Yale than one from Eastern Kentucky – unless, maybe, you're planning to live in eastern Kentucky after graduation – but it's true everywhere to some degree.)

While an individual might rationally pursue all three of these, only the first one – actual added skills – produces a net benefit for society. The other two are just distributional: They're about who gets the goodies, not about making more of them.

Yet today's college education system seems to be in the business of selling parts two and three to a much greater degree than part one, along with selling the even harder to quantify "college experience," which often boils down to four (or more) years of partying.

Post-bubble, perhaps students – and employers, not to mention parents and lenders – will focus instead on education that fosters economic value. And that is likely to press colleges to focus more on providing useful majors. (That doesn't necessarily rule out traditional liberal-arts majors, so long as they are rigorous and require a real general education rather than trendy and easy subjects, but the key word here is *rigorous*.)

My question is whether traditional academic institutions will be able to keep up with the times, or whether – as Anya Kamenetz suggests in her new book, *DIY U* – the real pioneering will be in online education and the work of "edupunks" who are more interested in finding new ways of teaching and learning than in protecting existing interests.

I'm betting on the latter. Industries seldom reform themselves, and real competition usually comes from the outside.

In this Broadside, we'll look briefly at how the higher education bubble came to be, at the problems it is creating, and about what is likely to happen when, and after, the bursting takes place. We'll also look at a few things you can do for yourself and for the country.

* * *

II. How We Got Here

Higher education has been around for a long time. The University of Bologna was started in 1088, and many other European universities date from the 12th, 13th, and 14th centuries. It has been a presence in the United States from the very earliest days of colonization – long enough ago that Harvard University supposedly once offered Galileo a job. But for most of that time, a college education, to say nothing of graduate study, was a luxury: Colleges and universities catered mostly to the rich and to the clergy, with the occasional deserving scholarship student thrown in.

College was not seen as the primary way for a young man (it was pretty much always a young man back then) to get ahead, at least not unless the young man was planning a career as a man of the cloth. Most lawyers – and even most doctors – learned more through apprenticeship and on-the-job training than through formal education, which is not surprising since that was the way most people, from blacksmiths to generals, learned what they needed to know for their jobs.

Instead, a college education was mostly a way for a young man of distinction to obtain a degree of social polish – and wider social connections – while sowing a few discreet (or sometimes not so discreet) wild oats. College was not sold as an economic investment in the future but rather as a stage in life, and no one was handing out loans to aspiring entrants.

This began to change after the Civil War, and the reason was, naturally enough, federal money. Even before the Civil War, reformer Justin Morrill had talked up the idea of colleges and universities dedicated to training farmers, mechanics, and soldiers rather than clergymen and lawyers. Morrill's original scheme involved colleges modeled on West Point, with free tuition and admission via congressional nomination. This proposal went through several different versions, one of which was vetoed by President James Buchanan on the eve of the Civil War, but a later bill was signed into law by Abraham Lincoln.

> *Total student-loan debt in America has passed the trillion-dollar mark, more than total credit-card debt and more than total auto-loan debt.*

As it was finally passed, the Morrill Act offered land grants to institutions that would offer education in farming and mechanics, along with a spot of military training. Though the traditional colleges looked down on these upstarts as little better than trade schools, many became elite universities such as Virginia Tech, Texas A&M, the University of Tennessee, the University of Wisconsin, MIT, and Cornell. Historians now regard the Morrill Act as a major step forward in education and a major booster for the U.S. economy, and many believe that the (then required) military training played a major role in

America's success in World Wars I and II.

Well, if some is good, more must be better. That was the thinking after World War II, when policymakers – wondering how to receive a flood of returning GIs – hit upon the idea of sending them to college. The GI Bill gave millions of discharged soldiers the option to go to school instead of hitting the job market all at once. Many took advantage of it, and colleges and universities, anxious to accommodate them (and to share in the federal largesse), embarked upon ambitious programs of expansion.

By the time the flood of veterans from World War II and Korea was slowing to a trickle, the Baby Boomers were beginning to show up, and the Vietnam War soon added yet another reason for college: student draft deferments. Enrollments swelled again, and colleges expanded further. By the 1970s, the infrastructure was there for more college students than the population was ready to produce on its own. The solution? Expanded federal aid in the form of Pell Grants, guaranteed student loans, and other support. This really took off in the mid- to late 1970s.

The result was predictable. As with any subsidized product, prices rose to absorb the subsidy. And as colleges saw that increases in tuition didn't hurt enrollment – higher tuition often made a school seem more prestigious, and anyway there were cheap government loans to make up the difference – the rate of increase climbed even further. How much further? Just look at the graphic on page 13, adapted from Professor Mark Perry at the Carpe Diem economics blog.

As you can see, at an annual growth rate of 7.45 percent a year, tuition has vastly outstripped the consumer price index and health care prices, while the growth in house prices under the housing bubble looks like a mere bump in the road by comparison. For a while, parents could look to increased home values to make them feel better about paying Junior's tuition (the so-called wealth effect, in which increases in asset values make people more comfortable about spending) or could at least

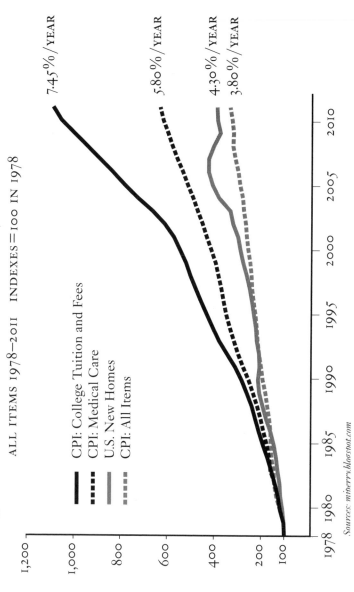

College Tuition *vs.* Medical Care *vs.* Home Prices *vs.* CPI

ALL ITEMS 1978–2011   INDEXES=100 IN 1978

7.45%/YEAR

5.80%/YEAR

4.30%/YEAR

3.80%/YEAR

CPI: College Tuition and Fees
CPI: Medical Care
U.S. New Homes
CPI: All Items

Sources: mjperry.blogspot.com

borrow against the equity in their homes to fund tuition. But that equity is gone now, and tuition is still climbing.

So where does that leave us? Even students who major in programs shown to increase earnings, like engineering, face limits to how much debt they can sanely amass. With costs approaching $60,000 a year for many private schools and out-of-state costs at many state schools exceeding $40,000 (and often closing in on $30,000 for in-state students), some people are graduating with debts of $100,000 or more – sometimes much more.

That's dangerous. And the problem is not a small one: According to Professor Richard Vedder, writing in the *Chronicle of Higher Education*, the number of student-loan debtors actually equals the number of people with college degrees. How is this possible? "First, huge numbers of those borrowing money *never* graduate from college. Second, many who borrow are not in baccalaureate degree programs. Three, people take forever to pay their loans back." Total student-loan debt in

America has passed the trillion-dollar mark, more than total credit-card debt and more than total auto-loan debt.

The rule of thumb is that college-debt payments should account for less than 8 percent of gross income. Otherwise, watch out – and remember that loan payments are usually not dischargeable in bankruptcy. The loans can follow you for decades. Students

---

The whole scheme seems like the debt-slavery regimes used by coal mines and plantations to keep workers and sharecroppers in debt peonage for life.

---

graduating with heavy burdens of student-loan debt must choose (if they can) jobs that pay enough money to cover the payments, often limiting their career choices to an extent they didn't foresee in their student days. And even students who can earn enough to service their debts may find themselves constrained in other ways. It's hard to get a mortgage, for example, when you're already in effect paying one in the form of student loans. (This has implications for the housing bubble too, of course, since the traditional source of new home buyers and move-up home buyers – people a few years out of college or grad school – now suffers from an unprecedented debt burden. But that's a topic for a different book.)

It's even worse, of course, when graduates *can't* find jobs that will let them cover the payments. Regardless of the student's employment circumstances, the debt still comes due. Students can enter forbearance, but that only reduces or stops the payments for a while; the principal continues to grow. Only death or (sometimes) disability will get rid of the debt, and for private student loans, co-signers may remain liable. The whole scheme, as several commentators have noted, seems like the debt-slavery regimes used by coal mines and plantations to keep workers and sharecroppers in debt peonage for life. (Some newer graduates may be eligible for "income-based repayment" schemes, which make things somewhat better, but not much.)

For some of these unfortunates, the debt is enough to quash marriage plans (who wants to marry someone with huge amounts of unpayable debt?), prevent homeownership, and generally wreak havoc on the debtors' lives. These people may wind up living in their parents' basements until they are old enough to collect Social Security, which may wind up being garnisheed – no joke – for unpaid student debts.

It's a big problem, and more and more students and potential students are becoming aware of just how bad student debt can be. That's causing them to change their behavior. Some are eschewing college entirely in favor of military service, skilled trades, or lower-cost alternatives like community college. Others are skipping expensive private colleges (especially those outside the top tier) in favor of less expensive state schools. Some are pursuing their educations online. And even those still going to traditional colleges or universities are looking more closely at their majors and the employment prospects after graduation. Nor are graduate programs immune: The number of students taking the Law School Admissions Test, for example, has fallen by 25 percent over the past two years, leading some to predict that lower-tier law schools may be entering a "death spiral."

These are all rational responses to the fact that the traditional approach to higher education no longer makes as much sense. When education was cheap enough that students could pay their own way through by working part time, "study what interests you" was reasonable advice. Some criticize today's students for being more concerned about return on investment, but when the investment runs well into six figures, students would be crazy *not* to worry about the return. A six-figure consumption item is well beyond the resources of college students: Nobody would advise an 18-year-old to purchase a Ferrari on borrowed money, but if a college education is a consumption item, not an investment, that's basically what they are doing.

But as the behavior that led to the bubble changes, the bubble itself will burst, and things in the higher education world will never be quite the same. That has significant ramifications for both students and institutions. The next chapter looks at some of those.

III. What Happens When the Bubble Bursts?

For the past several decades, higher education has been living high on the hog. Faculty salaries have grown significantly, administrative salaries have grown dramatically – seven-figure pay for university presidents isn't even news any more, and at most schools, there are scores of lower-level officials who still make more money than anyone else on campus except coaches – and institutions of higher

Some criticize today's students for being more concerned about return on investment, but when the investment runs well into six figures, students would be crazy not to worry about the return.

learning have been on a building boom, running up new administration buildings, athletic facilities, dormitories, recreation centers, and classrooms.

All of this is predicated on the money continuing to roll in. But what if it stops? Already, state and local aid to higher education is shrinking as states face pension shortfalls and other budget pressures. State and local spending on higher education hit a 25-year low in 2011, and nothing suggests a significant upturn in years to come. Schools have tried to make up the difference by raising tuition, but for the first time, we're beginning to see significant buyer resistance. Federal money is still there, but it's not growing the way it once was, and with the federal government running massive deficits, the prospects for its filling the gap also seem poor. So what will happen?

At first, of course, the answer will mostly be denial: short-term solutions, efforts to raise quick cash, and a suggestion that what's going on is just temporary. Later there will be more-significant changes, mostly aimed at cost cutting. (If experience is any guide, administration – especially sacred cows like diversity programs – will be cut last; actual teaching will be cut first.) Finally, there will be mergers and even outright closings of schools that can no longer operate. The schools that are left will be those that can survive in the new environment.

This won't be the end of higher education, of course, and the schools at the top of the food chain – the Ivy League and similar schools; top engineering schools like MIT, CalTech, and Georgia Tech; and the better flagship public universities – will survive comparatively unscathed. But the transformation will nonetheless be wrenching. Less-expensive alternative-education and certification schemes will arise, and existing institutions will do their best to marginalize and neutralize them by employing everything from PR offensives to accrediting powers to outright legal assaults, but over time those assaults will largely fail.

We're already seeing some of this. Even as the once-mighty University of California system slashes programs and raises tuition, it has created a new systemwide "vice chancellor for equity, diversity, and inclusion." This is on top of the already enormous University of California diversity machine, which, as Heather Mac Donald notes, "includes the Chancellor's Diversity Office, the associate vice chancellor for faculty equity, the assistant vice chancellor for diversity, the faculty equity advisors, the graduate diversity coordinators, the staff diversity liaison, the under-graduate student diversity liaison, the graduate student diversity liaison, the chief diversity officer, the director of development for diversity initiatives, the Office of Academic Diversity and Equal Opportunity, the Committee on Gender Identity and Sexual Orientation Issues, the Committee on the Status of Women, the Campus Council on Climate, Culture and Inclusion, the Diversity Council, and the directors of the Cross-Cultural Center, the Lesbian Gay Bisexual Transgender Resource Center, and the Women's Center."

While the UC system loses top cancer researchers to Rice University, it is creating new chaired professorships in, you guessed it, diversity studies. Likewise, in North Carolina, UNC-Wilmington is combining the physics and geology departments to save money while diverting more funding to campus diversity offices. This sort of thing illustrates the kind of priorities that emerge in a bubble that is not only financial but also intellectual. It will not survive in the new environment, though administrators will fight a grim rear-guard action as long as they are allowed, even though research suggests that the programs aren't doing much good – as students grow less, not more, committed to racial and gender equality the longer they are in college. (Read more on what to do about that administrative resistance in a later chapter.)

For a time, many schools will try to maintain their enrollments by discounting tuition – usually disguised as increased financial aid – but there are limits to that approach. First of all, to the extent that they need tuition money to survive, schools won't be able to afford these discounts for long. Second, as more schools adopt this strategy, we're likely to see a race to the bottom. And third, once word of heavy discounting gets out, parents who are expected to pay full freight will feel like suckers and either demand discounts for themselves or take their business elsewhere.

For the most vulnerable schools, the problem won't be one of priorities but of survival. Generally speaking, the most-vulnerable schools will be those private schools with modest reputations and limited endowments but with high tuitions. A generation or two in the past, such schools could maintain enrollment via legacies or, in some cases, religious affiliations. But when you're nearly as expensive as (or even more expensive than) Harvard but lack the reputation of Harvard, attracting students won't be as easy. And since schools with modest endowments can't supplement tuition income with endowment income, there will be sharp limits to their ability to cut their prices anyway, at least without engaging in dramatic cost cutting first. In my own world – legal education – some fourth-tier schools that had plenty of applicants a few years ago are already having trouble filling seats. That's just the beginning.

The upshot is that higher education is facing a major structural change over the next decade or so, and the full impact is likely to strike sooner than most people expect. Change is coming, and it is unlikely to be either modest or gradual.

But how should people prepare for this change? Assume that I'm right, and that higher education – both undergraduate and graduate, including professional education like the law schools in which I teach – is heading for a major correction. What will that mean? What should people do?

IV. What to Do

Piece of advice No. 1 – good for pretty much all bubbles, in fact – is this: Don't go into debt. In bubbles, people borrow heavily because they expect the value of what they're borrowing against to increase. In a booming housing market, for example, it makes sense to buy a house you can't quite afford, because it will increase in value enough to make the debt seem trivial, or at least manageable, so long as the market continues to boom. But there's a catch. Once the boom is over, all that debt is still there, but the return thereon is much diminished. And since the boom is based on expectations, things can go south with amazing speed once those expectations start to shift.

Right now, people are still borrowing heavily to pay the steadily increasing tuitions levied by higher education. But that borrow-

---

My advice to students:
Don't go to colleges or schools
that will require you to borrow
a lot of money to attend.

---

ing is based on the expectation that students will earn enough to pay off their loans with a portion of the extra income their educations generate. Once people doubt that will happen, the bubble will burst. And there's considerable evidence that the doubting is already well under way.

So my advice to students faced with choosing colleges (and graduate schools and law schools) this coming year is simple: Don't go to colleges or schools that will require you to borrow a lot of money to attend. There's a good chance you'll find yourself deep in debt for no purpose. On the other hand, all that tuition discounting may mean that there will be bargains to be had. Just don't expect them to always be obvious bargains; you may have to research, and even dicker a bit, to get the best deal. Don't be afraid to dicker. Schools may act like that's unheard of, but you won't be the only one.

And maybe you should rethink college entirely. According to a recent report in *The Washington Post*, many people with college educations are already jumping the tracks to become skilled manual laborers: plumbers, electricians, and the like. And the Bureau of Labor Statistics predicts that 7 of the 10 fastest-growing jobs in the next decade will be based on on-the-job training rather than higher education. (And they'll be hands-on jobs that

ENCOUNTER 🔫 BROADSIDES®

AMMUNITION FOR SERIOUS DEBATE.

Available as eBooks
visit our website at www.encounterbooks.com

To order, contact Perseus Distribution
at 1-800-343-4499; or email
orderentry@perseusbooks.com

For Publicity, contact Lauren Miklos
at 212-871-5741; or email
lmiklos@encounterbooks.com

are hard to outsource to foreigners: If you want your toilet fixed, it can't be done by somebody in Bangalore). If the *Post* is right about this trend, a bursting of the bubble is growing likelier.

What about higher education folks? What should they (er, we) do? Well, once again, what can't go on forever, won't.

For the past several decades, colleges and universities have built endowments, played *Moneyball*-style faculty-hiring games, and constructed grand new buildings while jacking up tuitions to pay for all these things (and, in the case of state schools, to make up for gradually diminishing public support). That has been made possible by an ocean of money borrowed by students – often with the encouragement and assistance of the universities. Business plans that are based on the continuation of this borrowing are likely to fare poorly.

Just as I advised students not to go into debt, my advice to universities is similar: Don't go on spending binges now that you expect to pay for with tuition revenues (or government aid) later. Those revenues may not be there as expected. Some colleges have already gotten in trouble by borrowing money in the debt markets to support capital improvements that state funding won't pay for, only to face difficulty paying the money back. Expect more of this down the line unless my advice is followed.

If higher education is going to justify its cost, there needs to be much more return on investment, which means much more actual learning.

It's also time to think about curriculum reform and changes in instructional methods. Post-bubble, students are likely to be far more concerned about getting actual value for their educational dollars. Faced with straitened circumstances, colleges and universities will have to look at cutting costs while simultaneously increasing quality.

Online education and programs that focus more on things that can help students' earnings than on what the faculty want to teach will help deliver more value for the dollar. In some areas, we may even see a move to apprenticeship models or other approaches that provide more-genuine skills upon graduation.

The first step is to ensure that students are actually learning useful things. This isn't much of a problem in engineering schools and the like, but in many other areas, core subjects have been shortchanged. A recent survey of more than 700 schools by the American Council of Trustees and Alumni found that many have virtually no requirements. Perhaps that's why students are studying 50 percent less than they were a couple of decades ago.

A recent book, *Academically Adrift*, by Richard Arum and Josipa Roksa, surveyed college students and found that there wasn't a lot of learning going on:

45 percent of students "did not demonstrate any significant improvement in learning" during the first two years of college.

36 percent of students "did not demonstrate any significant improvement in learning" over four years of college.

Prices have been going up, but learning seems to have been going down. The primary reason, according to the study, is that courses aren't very rigorous. There's not much required of students, and the students aren't doing more than is required. If higher education is going to justify its cost, there needs to be much more return on investment, which means much more actual learning, which means more-rigorous course content and less fluff.

Once this issue is addressed, there's plenty of room for improvement on the technological front. In the old days, professors were few, and it made sense for students to travel hundreds of miles to study with them. But today, once you move onto a campus, much of your learning, especially in the first couple of years, takes place in huge lecture halls where one professor addresses hundreds of students – or gets a teaching assistant to do it.

Some students are saving money by doing their first two years at community college. The quality of instruction is often better, and the classes smaller, than in four-year institutions where professors focus more on research than on teaching.

That's a worthwhile strategy, but innovation at four-year institutions could help too. Now that webcasts are a routine feature of corporate training, perhaps it's time to make better use of the Web for education. Take the top teachers in a field and let students at multiple colleges access their lectures online. (Sure, there's not a lot of one-on-one interaction that way – but how much is there in a 200-student lecture class, really?) Once the basic information is covered, students can apply it in person in smaller advanced classes. Would this save money? Possibly – and it would almost certainly produce better results.

The online approach is used by the popular

Khan Academy, where students view lectures at their convenience and perfect their skills via video-game-like software, and the follow-up is done in a classroom with a teacher's oversight. The idea is to take advantage of mass delivery when it works best and allow individualized attention when it helps most.

The Khan Academy has gotten a lot of attention, but it's not the last word in technological progress in education. Many for-profit online schools, like Kaplan or Strayer University, are using their standardized course content and large enrollments to perform deep statistical analysis of how students perform and how changes in course content and course presentation can improve learning. This is a knowledge base that is unavailable to traditional universities.

What's striking is that most of the potentially revolutionary change we're seeing has come from outside the educational establishment. Then again, breakthroughs often come from people working outside the old industries. Kamenetz's book *DIY U* talks about "edupunks" who are exploring unconventional thinking about teaching and learning. In fact, the best way to master many subjects may be for students to find their own path, with the role of the education establishment being more to certify competence than to actually teach. In one way, that's how it works already.

College now serves largely as a status marker, a sign of membership in the educated "caste," and as a place for people to meet future spouses of commensurate status.

Right now, a college degree is an expensive signifier that its holder has a basic ability to show up on time (mostly), to follow instructions (reasonably well), and to deal with others in close quarters without committing serious felonies. In some fields, it may also indicate important background knowledge and skills, but most students will require further on-the-job training. An institution that could provide similar certification without requiring four (or more) years and a six-figure investment would have a huge advantage, especially if employers found that certification to be a more reliable indicator of competence than a college degree. Couple that with apprenticeship programs or internships, and you might not need college for many careers.

The major problem with this plan is that college now serves largely as a status marker, a sign of membership in the educated "caste," and as a place for people to meet future spouses of commensurate status. However, the sight of college graduates buried in debt may change that. We're already seeing signs of a shift in popular culture, with advice columns and news articles appearing that discuss women and men whose huge student debt makes them unmarriageable. At any rate,

American culture at its best values people more for what they do than for their membership in a caste – and now seems like a good time to reassert that preference.

Perhaps online programs from prestigious schools will bridge the gap. MIT has already put many of its courses online. At present, you can learn from them, and even get certification, but there's no degree attached. It wouldn't be hard for MIT to add standard exams and a diploma, though, and if they do it right, an online degree from MIT might be worth a lot – not as much as an old-fashioned MIT degree, perhaps, but quite possibly more than a degree from many existing brick-and-mortar schools. We're beginning to see the beginnings of this with accredited schools like Western Governors University. There's also a new online start-up, Minerva University, that aims to compete with elite brick-and-mortar schools, and it includes such big names as former Harvard president Larry Summers.

Meanwhile, for the states and big donors

who fund those portions of higher education that the students don't, a post-bubble world will bring some changes too. Many states have been cutting aid to higher education, content to let higher tuition pick up the slack. Some may choose to change that (if they can afford it), but regardless, I expect more direct oversight of state institutions from those who fund them. Universities' priorities will be brought closer to states' priorities, and we can expect more outside pressure for increased rigor and fewer courses and majors in areas that seem to be more about politics or trendiness than substance. We can also expect resistance from those with investments in those fields, but it is unlikely to prevail as the money runs out.

For private schools, government oversight is less direct – but to an even greater extent than state schools, private institutions have been dependent on a flood of government-guaranteed credit, and they are likely to see more scrutiny as well if that is to continue.

As former British Prime Minister Margaret Thatcher famously remarked, the problem with socialism is that you eventually run out of other people's money, and that's likely to be the problem facing higher education too: not enough of other people's money.

Graduation rates, employment after graduation, loan-default rates, and so on are likely to get a lot more attention. Institutions may even be forced to absorb some of the cost of student-loan defaults as an incentive to encourage students to not take on more debt than they can repay or to major in fields in which employment prospects are dim.

Finally, for the entrepreneurs out there, this bubble's bursting may be an opportunity. One of the underpinnings of higher education, as mentioned above, is its value as a credential to employers. A college degree demonstrates at least moderate intelligence and, more important, the ability to show up and perform on a reasonably reliable basis, something that is of considerable interest when hiring people, a surprisingly large number of whom (as most employers can attest) do neither.

But a college degree is an expensive way to get an entry-level credential. New approaches to credentialing, approaches that inform employers more reliably while costing less than a college degree, are likely to become increasingly appealing over the coming decade.

If I were an employer, I'd find a reliable non-college-based credentialing system pretty appealing. First, it wouldn't have to be all that great to be a more-reliable indicator of knowledge and skills than a typical college diploma. Second, all things being equal, I'd much rather hire someone who wasn't burdened by six-figure debt. Such employees are likely to be more cheerful, less financially stressed (which can lead to problems with embezzlement and worse) and, significantly, willing to work for less since they don't have big student-loan payments to cover.

What's more, someone who successfully completes a rigorous program online is likely to be more self-disciplined, more of a self-starter, than someone who completes college in the traditional fashion. For a lot of employers, that's sure to be a significant plus.

So there's a need for an alternative credentialing system. Filling that need will make someone rich. To any entrepreneurs reading this, good luck – and once you hit it big, please remember the impecunious law professor who put this idea in your head.

V. Politics

Wrenching economic change is easy to endure, so long as it's happening to other people. Thus, as blue-collar workers suffered the pangs of economic transitions in the 1980s and 1990s, it was easy for white-collar workers and academics to talk about the benefits of globalization and of technological progress in the workplace. They may have been right about all that, but don't expect academics to be so enthusiastic when their jobs are being eliminated and their pay is being cut.

The bursting of the higher education

bubble is pretty much inevitable, a product of economic forces that politics cannot control. But that doesn't mean that there won't be a political firestorm or two along the way. And while politics won't prevent the bubble from bursting, the political response can make a big difference in how well things go. What kinds of responses can we expect?

At one end of the spectrum, we may see the sort of die-hard job protection that we've seen in other shrinking sectors, where the focus is on (1) keeping competition down for as long as possible; and (2) preserving the jobs, perks, and salaries of senior workers at all costs. If that is the main response, we'll see bitterly contested efforts to use accrediting agencies and other gatekeepers to block the rise of new, lower-cost approaches to higher education. At the same time, we'll see existing tenured faculty fighting to retain their positions, while new academic hires become non-tenure-track contract appointments. (Already, many universities have turned many or most introductory courses over to low-paid adjuncts or visiting professors who don't have tenure and in many cases don't get health or retirement benefits.) In the short term, this will reduce the pain for faculty members and administrators, but the end result will be a hollowed-out university.

At the other end, we may see serious efforts to rebuild the higher education model. Instead of looking at what faculty want and then telling students that's what they get, we may instead look at what skills and knowledge students need to possess at graduation – and can afford to pay for – and structure programs accordingly.

In practice, of course, it won't be an either/or thing: Because higher education is decentralized, we'll see all sorts of different responses. Some will succeed and some will fail. Those who learn from the experience of others will be better able to make their own choices. Those who don blinders will learn only from their own experience, which may well turn out to be bitter.

Where state institutions are concerned,

there will be an opportunity for the public to take a hand, if people are interested. Ordinarily, running state universities is left to administrators and trustees, with perhaps a bit of attention from the legislature, mostly where budgets are concerned. But as things begin to change, new ideas from outside will get a hearing.

Interested citizens should consider attending trustees meetings, talking to legislators, and in general making noise about the priorities of state institutions and whether or not they are serving the public. Does it make sense to cut science funding while expanding diversity programs? Is a new gym or stadium really a top priority? It is quite possible that we will see a broad-based popular movement for higher education reform. University spokespeople have been telling us for years that higher education is a matter of public interest. It should not be surprising if the public becomes interested as it becomes clear that the existing model has failed. My advice to outside agitators: Master the arcana of the

The higher education bubble isn't bursting because of a shortage of money. It is bursting because of a shortage of value.

budget process. Even many university administrators don't really understand how it works.

Private institutions do not enjoy (if that is the word) the same degree of outside scrutiny – but here, too, alumni, students, parents, and other interested parties will have more of a chance to weigh in than has been usual. And given that private institutions are actually more dependent on federal student-loan money than state institutions are, they will be particularly subject to pressures for reform that are tied to eligibility to receive federal funds.

Students and prospective students will have an effect – and, indeed, already are doing so – simply by becoming better informed and less willing to pay top dollar for an inferior product. Ultimately, you can't run a college if you can't fill the seats with paying students, and that will be harder and harder to do for schools that don't produce visible value. The schools that get ahead of the curve will prosper, while those that lag behind will not.

There will likely be at least one major effort to secure federal bailout money for the higher education sector, but the prospects for that relief seem poor. The nation is already in sad financial shape, and higher education already received a substantial slug of "stimulus" money in 2009 that was mostly used to conduct business as usual for a bit longer.

The higher education bubble isn't bursting because of a shortage of money. It is bursting because of a shortage of value. The solution is to improve the product, not to increase the subsidy.

*   *   *

Conclusion

There's nothing evil or unnatural about a bubble or about the people who participate in one. Bubbles are an inevitable part of human nature and appear in almost every field of endeavor. When bubbles burst it's painful – but the sources of the pain lie not so much in the bust as in the poor decisions made during the preceding boom. Resources were allocated in ways that didn't make sense, because the bubble made them *seem* to make sense for a while. The consequences of that misallocation account for the pain.

And it's not the end of the world when a bubble bursts, either. When the tech bubble burst, people lost money (some people lost a *lot* of money) and some people lost jobs, but the Internet didn't go away, and neither did Internet businesses. Likewise, the bursting of the higher education bubble won't mean the end of higher education. It'll just mean that there will be less "dumb money" out there to be harvested.

But inevitably, change will come, and that's not so bad. This is the 21st century. It's not shocking to think that higher education will go through major changes over the coming decade or two. What would be shocking would be if things stayed the same, when rapid change has been the norm lately in every other knowledge-based industry.

I don't pretend to know how it will all work out, but I hope the thoughts in this Broadside have been useful to readers, and I encourage you to join in the conversation in the years to come.

Copyright © 2012 by Glenn Harlan Reynolds

First American edition published in 2012 by Encounter Books,
an activity of Encounter for Culture and Education, Inc.,
a nonprofit, tax exempt corporation.
Encounter Books website address: www.encounterbooks.com

Manufactured in the United States and printed on
acid-free paper. The paper used in this publication meets
the minimum requirements of ANSI/NISO z39.48 1992
(R 1997) (*Permanence of Paper*).

FIRST AMERICAN EDITION

LIBRARY OF CONGRESS CATALOGING-IN-PUBLICATION DATA

Reynolds, Glenn H.
The higher education bubble / by Glenn H. Reynolds.
p.   cm.
ISBN 978-1-59403-665-1 (pbk. : alk. paper)
ISBN 978-1-59403-666-8 (ebook)
1. Education, Higher—United States. 2. Educational change—
United States. 3. College costs—United States. I. Title.
LA227.4.R478 2012
378.73—dc23
2012015017

10 9 8 7 6 5 4 3 2 1

SERIES DESIGN BY CARL W. SCARBROUGH